34 CRAFT STICK PROJECTS

by
Michelle Graff
and
Loretta E. Reese

STANDARD PUBLISHING
Cincinnati, Ohio   2104

Illustrated by C. T. Cartland and Romilda Dilley

Library of Congress Catalog Card No. 82-61453

ISBN: 0-87239-622-3

Revised © 1983, The Standard Publishing Company, Cincinnati, Ohio
Division of Standex International Corporation
Printed in U.S.A.

TABLE OF CONTENTS

LARGE GIFT BOX

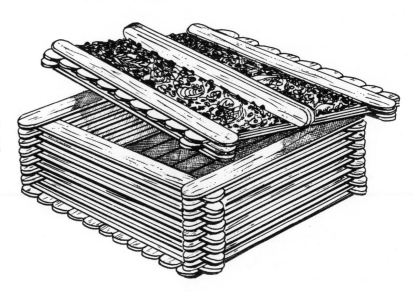

Trimmed with shells, beads, gravel, or tiny artificial flowers, this is an attractive box designed to hold just about anything from cuff links to paper clips on your dresser, desk, or coffee table.

Materials Needed:

70 sticks
4 small wooden beads

Directions:

Place 11 sticks on your working surface, side by side. Glue two sticks across them, one at each end, slightly in from the edges. These sticks form the base of the box.

Apply a dab of glue to each end of the cross sticks, and place two more across them in opposite directions. Continue building layers in this way until there are 16 layers (two sticks in each layer). You now have the lower part of the box. Glue a wooden bead to each corner of base for legs.

For lid, repeat procedure for the base, but make only four layers of two sticks each. Cut and glue four sticks to make lid fit securely (see illustration). Glue sticks to top of lid as shown above, and decorate.

NOTE: For a taller box, add more layers to lower part.

Base for box and lid

Lid—cut sticks to secure lid when on box

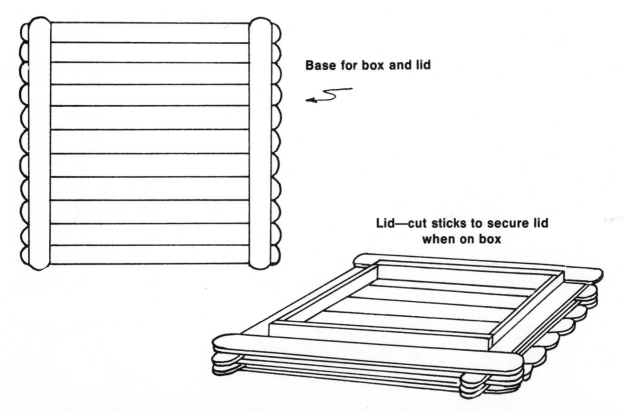

SUNBURST MAT

This mat is simple to make and very versatile. It can be used as a trivet or wall decoration, planter stand, backing for a wall clock, and many other things.

Left in its natural state, the mat is a very striking decoration; but the sticks can easily be dipped and dyed with paint or fabric colors, spattered with spray paint, or decorated with brush designs. Make the mat even more festive for holiday use by spraying with metallic paint.

Materials Needed:

33 small (⅜″) wooden beads, plain or colored
33 sticks, drilled as shown
1 yard of elastic for threading beads and sticks

Directions:

Drill holes in all sticks, as shown. Thread the elastic through end holes in all sticks and pull tightly. Tie off neatly. Cut off excess elastic.

Thread another piece of elastic through center holes in sticks, adding beads between sticks to spread the mat into shape. Pull the elastic fairly tight (so the mat will still lie flat) and tie off. Cut off excess elastic.

NOTE: If you use ¼″ beads, you will need about 48 beads and sticks.

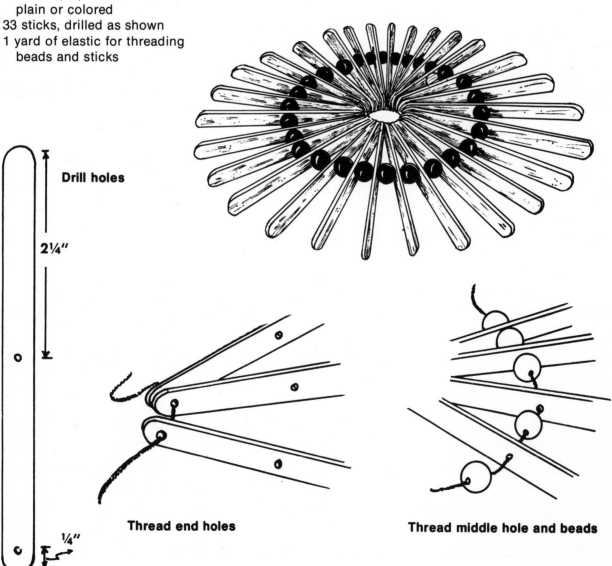

Drill holes

2¼″

¼″

Thread end holes

Thread middle hole and beads

WREN HOUSE

When Mr. and Mrs. Wren are busily looking for a home, they are looking for one neat and pretty—just like this one. With a coat of varnish or shellac, the little house is quite weatherproof and warm. Just the thing for honeymooners!

Materials Needed:

36 sticks
Cork—6″ x 3½″ x ¼″ thick

Directions:

Place 11 sticks side by side. These sticks form the floor of the wren house.

Cut triangles from the cork. Make a hole in one piece for birds to enter (see illustration, or use the pattern on page 45). Apply glue to the bottom edges of triangles and set crosswise onto the sticks, one at each end.

Apply glue to the remaining edges of the triangles and place sticks across them from side to side. Before adding the last two sticks at each side, add stick pieces cut and drilled as shown.

Glue these sticks close to the cork between the last two (top) sticks.

For a perch, glue two sticks side by side, to base.

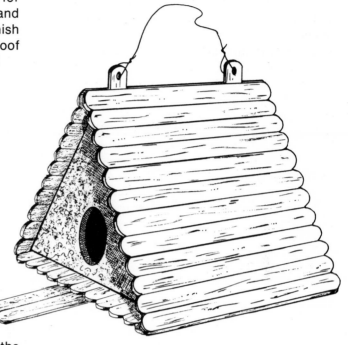

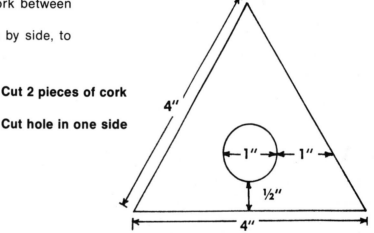

Cut 2 pieces of cork

Cut hole in one side

4″

1″   1″

½″

4″

Drill and cut for hanging

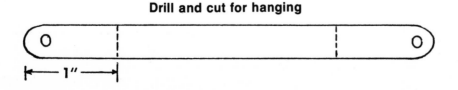

1″

HOT DISH MAT

Simple to make, this craft can be enjoyed by young children.

Materials Needed:

14 sticks
Burlap or felt (4⅝" x 4½")
Tempera paint or pieces of felt

Directions:

Glue 12 craft sticks side by side on the piece of material. Place under a heavy weight to dry.

Glue a stick near each end across the back.

Decorate with flowers cut from felt or designs painted with tempera paint.

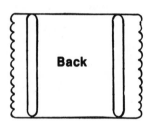
Back

LETTER/NAPKIN HOLDER

Whether you select this craft to be used as a letter holder or a napkin holder, you will be pleased with the result. Follow the colors suggested or choose your own. Carpenter's glue is recommended when working with wood.

Materials Needed:

15 craft sticks
Piece of wood 5" x 3½" x ¾"
Acrylic paints (blue, orange, yellow, brown, and green)
Black construction paper circle ½" in diameter
Carpenter's glue
Manila construction paper
Two ¼" diameter beads
Toothpick
#484 Tacky cement

Directions:

Cut eight craft sticks as shown (see A). Paint green the eight cut sticks and four uncut sticks. Paint the wood block green.

When dry, glue six sticks together to form fence (see B). Make two. Attach fence pieces to

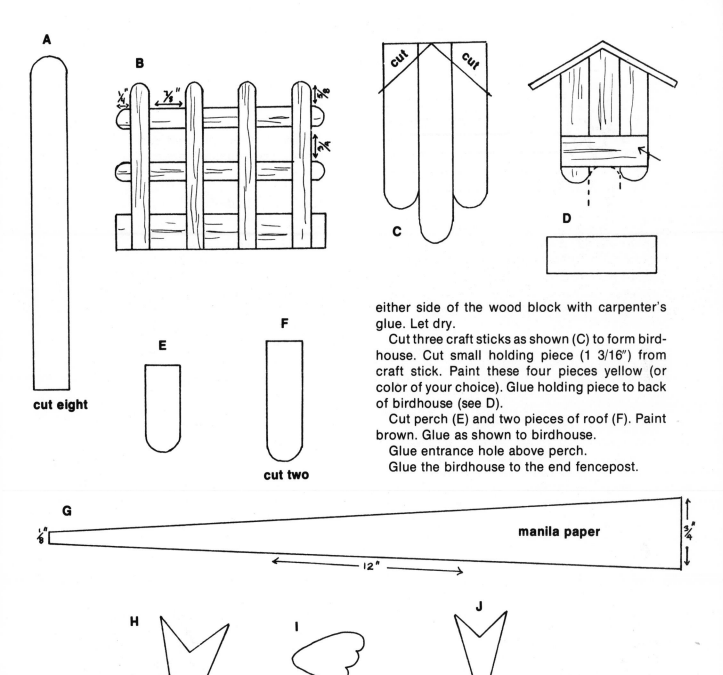

A

cut eight

B

C

D

E

F

cut two

either side of the wood block with carpenter's glue. Let dry.

Cut three craft sticks as shown (C) to form birdhouse. Cut small holding piece (1 3/16") from craft stick. Paint these four pieces yellow (or color of your choice). Glue holding piece to back of birdhouse (see D).

Cut perch (E) and two pieces of roof (F). Paint brown. Glue as shown to birdhouse.

Glue entrance hole above perch.

Glue the birdhouse to the end fencepost.

G

manila paper

H

bead head

bird body

toothpick

I

wing

cut 2

J

tail

diagramed (H) for the head and tail attachments.

Attach the bead onto the head end of the manila body with glue. Add a piece of toothpick to the bead to form the beak.

Cut the wings and tail from manila construction paper (see I and J). Attach with glue. Paint the birds blue. The female bird has light orange underneath. The male is all blue. Dot the eyes with yellow paint. Then add a black dot to center of yellow. Set the birds in place with a large drop of #484 Tacky cement. One bird is on the perch (female) and the other is on the roof.

For each bird (make two): Cut a piece of manila construction paper as shown (see G). Form the manila paper around a #3 double pointed knitting needle, starting at the large end. Tightly and evenly wind to the narrow end, sealing it with glue. This is the bird's body. Cut the body as

ECOLOGY PLAQUE

God created the world for us to live in. The ecology plaque shows us part of this world, and reminds us that we should keep our obligation to take care of this world.

Materials Needed:

22 sticks
Artificial flowers
Paint or shellac, optional
Picture made from felt or construction paper
Hanger

Directions:

Lay 18 sticks side by side to form a rectangular shape. Glue four sticks across these sticks, overlapping one end to bond all the sticks together. Allow to dry. This will form the backside.

At this point, the plaque can be painted or shellacked, if desired. Allow to dry.

Cut out the picture on page 45, or make one from felt or construction paper. To have a built-up effect, make another tree, bird, lion, and fish from construction paper or felt. Put a dot of silicone (or glue thickened with flour) on each small piece and position it on the same object in the picture. Do not press down on the pieces.

Position the picture, flowers, and Scripture verse on the plaque and glue down. Attach a hanger to the back so the ecology plaque can be hung on the wall.

NOTE HOUSE

When you have to make an emergency errand and have no way to get in touch with a neighbor or an expected friend, write a hasty note and leave it in this little house. A short pencil kept inside the note house will give your visitor a chance to reply, if necessary.

Materials Needed:

33 sticks
Two 1⅝″ x 5½″ pieces of plywood or cork, for sides
One 1⅝″ x 4¼″ piece of plywood or cork, for base
One wooden bead
One small hinge, cord, or metal paper rings, for door hinge

Directions:

Base: Cut two sides to pattern shown (B). Glue sides to base, about ¼″ in from the ends.

Sides: Cut one piece of plywood or cork to pattern shown (A).

Back: Glue 15 sticks across backs of side pieces.

Roof: Glue five sticks across slanted side pieces.

Door: Place nine sticks side by side. Glue a 3¼″ piece of stick across the center (to hold the other sticks together). When glue is dry, turn the sticks over and glue a cross stick, slantwise, across door.

Miter ends of two 3″ pieces of stick, and glue them across door.

Glue on the bead knob.

To finish: Drill two holes in the left side piece, one near roof and one near base. Drill corresponding holes in door. Fasten door on with metal rings or cord. (If you use a metal hinge, do not drill holes.)

Letter your family name and "Please Leave a Note" (see page 47) on door braces.

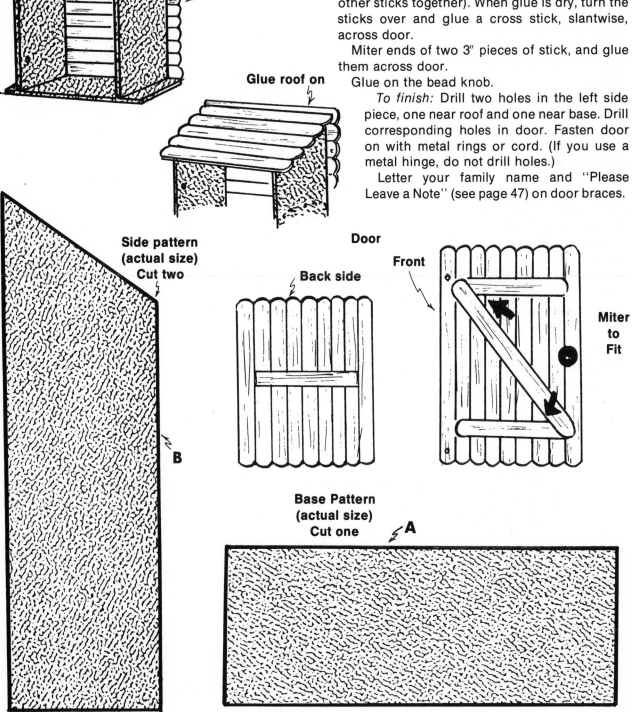

Glue side, base, and back together

Glue roof on

Side pattern (actual size) Cut two

B

Door

Back side

Front

Miter to Fit

Base Pattern (actual size) Cut one

A

FRUIT CART

Give a "touch of Paris" to a mantle or table top by filling this vendor's cart with tiny fruits.

Materials Needed:

58 sticks
4½" square cork (¼" thickness)

Directions:

For canopy, place eight sticks side by side lengthwise. Glue two sticks (see A) 1/16" in from edge. Cut two sticks to fit between (A) sticks and glue. See (B) sticks. Cut 1¼" pieces from each end of 20 sticks and glue these around (A) and (B) sticks to form drape effect.

For cart, place eight sticks side by side. For (C) and (D) sides, glue a small piece of stick to connect two sticks. Glue to base. Repeat. For (E) and (F) sides, glue small piece to two sticks and cut to fit across between (C) and (D) sides. Repeat.

For handle, glue two sticks as shown by (G) onto each side of base. Glue on two more as shown in finished illustration.

To attach wheels, turn base upside down and glue on two cross sticks. Cut four 2¼" diameter circles from the cork and cut slit in center. Push slit in circle over these sticks.

To connect the canopy to the cart, glue one stick to each inside corner as shown above.

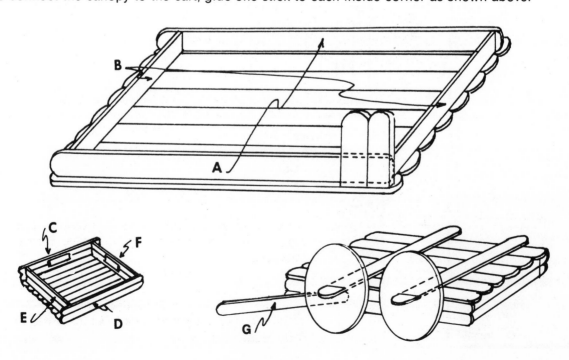

DOLLHOUSE FURNITURE

Delight a little girl with these replicas of real rustic furniture. You may want to make others for pretty knickknacks for your collection shelf.

Materials Needed:

Love seat—20 sticks
Picnic set—18 sticks
Dresser set—24 sticks
    Two 1½" x 2¼" pieces of cork ⅛" thick
    4 beads

Directions:

Love Seat

Back and sides: Glue nine sticks side by side in such a way that the top ends create a curved effect. Make sure the 1st, 5th, and 9th sticks are equal, since they will form legs to support the back of the chair (see illustration).

Place two 2" pieces of stick on each side of the back for armrest supports. Cement two sticks across these to hold all parts together.

Seat: Place three sticks side by side and glue short pieces of a stick crossways underneath to hold them together. Glue the seat to the back part, about 1¼" from the bottom. Glue a 2" piece of stick to the arm supports on each side.

Paint sticks and decorate with miniature designs.

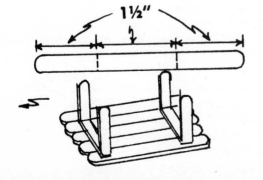

Picnic Set

Picnic table: Glue five sticks side by side. For legs, cut two sticks as shown, and glue across each end.

Picnic bench: Place three sticks side by side and glue them together, using short pieces of stick on the underside to reinforce them.

Glue four ¾" pieces of stick to each corner to form legs.

Dresser Set

Dresser: Glue 20 sticks around two cork sides to form box. Paint and add designs. Add tiny beads or buttons for drawer handles.

Mirror: Glue a frame of sticks to fit around a small purse mirror, a piece of glass, or aluminum foil.

TRAIN ENGINE

Sturdy, useful, and decorative, this train engine craft can be enjoyed by all age groups. The cab roof comes off to allow storage in cab.

Materials Needed:

25 craft sticks
4 craft sticks 3¾"
4 tongue depressors
2 snap-apart skill sticks
1 snap-apart skill stick (roof) 3½"
4 snap-apart skill sticks (cab decoration) 2⅜"
Acrylic paints (yellow, blue, red, and black)
2 peaks from pulp egg cartons (1⅛" high and 1½" high)
Two construction paper windows 1½" x 1"
Two construction paper windows 1¼" x ¾"
Cardboard paper tube 4" long and 1½" in diameter
4" x 3½" corrugated cardboard (roof)
4 double-thick corrugated cardboard half wheels
2 corrugated cardboard pieces for cab
2 corrugated cardboard pieces for cab roof

Directions:

Using patterns (see A-D), cut out pieces needed from corrugated cardboard.

Paint all craft sticks and tongue depressors blue. Paint all snap-apart skill sticks yellow. Paint the tallest stack (from egg carton) yellow and the shortest one red. Paint all four wheels yellow. Paint the wheel tread black. Paint the corrugated roof section red.

Glue 13 craft sticks around the cardboard tube, keeping the ends flush with the bottom of the tube at one end.

Glue two tongue depressors together by the narrow edge to form a broad base to build the train.

Cut a circle from corrugated cardboard to fit over the tube. (The craft sticks are extended beyond the tube on one end, so the cardboard circle will fit within the craft sticks. See E.)

Glue two tongue depressors, one lengthwise and perpendicular to each side of the two lying side by side (see F).

Glue the tube to the bottom tongue depressors so the closed end of the tube extends beyond the end of the tongue depressors 1⅛".

Go to the opposite end of the tube and glue six craft sticks to the sides of the tongue depressors. Craft sticks should fit side by side, but not overlap.

On the inside of the rows of six craft sticks, glue one cut off craft stick (3¾") to the first and last stick on each side. The cut-off part of the sticks should rest on the tongue depressors. This will make an even wall on the inside to glue the two cardboard pieces (see G).

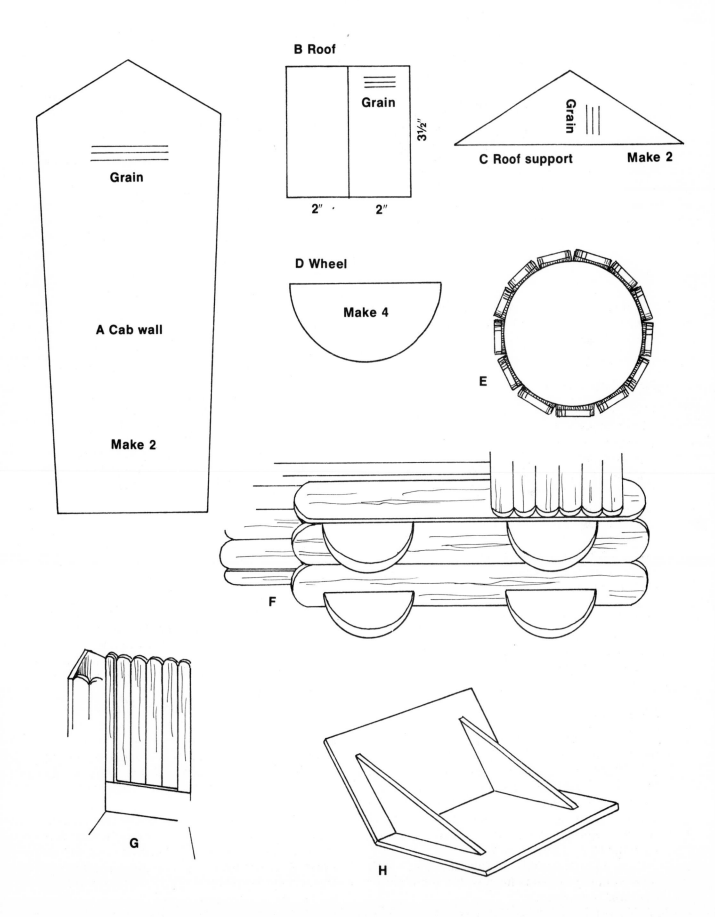

B Roof

Grain

3½"

2"   2"

C Roof support   Make 2

Grain

Grain

A Cab wall

Make 2

D Wheel

Make 4

E

F

G

H

15

CHURCH BANK

This little bank will help teach the importance of giving to God. Easy to make, it will hold each week's offering until church time. What better reminder to young and old alike that "God loves a cheerful giver"!

Materials Needed:

43 sticks
6½" x 3" x ¼" piece of cork
Scripture verse (1 Corinthians 16:2 or 2 Corinthians 9:7) written on strip of paper

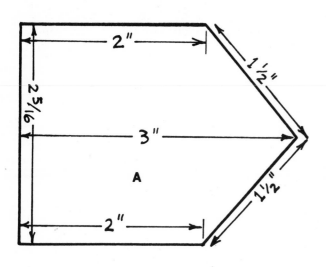

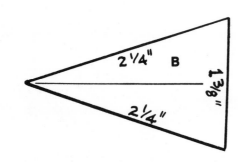

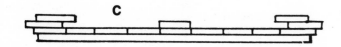

Directions:

Cut the two end panels and the steeple from cork by using the patterns provided (see A and B).

Lay seven sticks side by side. These sticks become the bottom of the bank.

Lay a line of glue across the sticks about ½" from each end and place the cork ends into position. Remove the center stick for coin removal.

Glue eight sticks into place on the top part of cork pieces for roof rafters. Begin gluing at the top. Before gluing the top stick, cut a slot in it for coins.

Build the side walls of the church to five sticks high, gluing the sticks in place one at a time. Notch the top sticks to fit around the roof rafters before gluing.

Cut notch in cork steeple to fit roof and glue into place. Cut small pieces of sticks for windows and doors, and glue into place.

For the sliding bottom, lay nine sticks side by side (see C).

Spread a line of glue across the sticks about 1" from each end and place two cross sticks into position. Let dry. Trim cross pieces.

Turn sticks over and glue one stick flat on each of two edges. Place them far enough apart so that the church may be slid between them.

Glue another stick flat on each of two edges, but this time offset the stick to the inside so that it will overlap the church base.

On the center stick of the sliding bottom, glue the stick taken from the church base for coin removal.

When glue is dry, slide bottom onto church.

Glue Scripture verse on roof of church.

HANDI-HOLDER

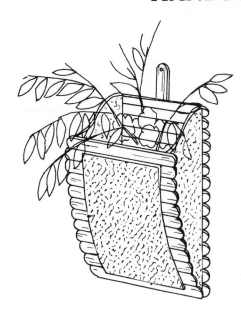

Here is just the thing for your family room, kitchen, or front porch. This useful holder will take care of that "in case I forget" or "remember to" note written to jog the memory of someone in your family. And what mother wouldn't just love to tuck her favorite recipes away here for a handy reference?

To make a decorative note holder, glue to the front of the sticks a 2½" x 3½" piece of cork and stick in push pins. Fill holder with artificial flowers or ferns.

Materials Needed:

31 sticks
6" x 3" piece of cork, ¼" thick
2½" x 3½" piece of cord 1/16" thick

Directions:

Place cork on a hard surface and cut out two side pieces, using the pattern on page 19.

Place 16 sticks side by side on table (for back of holder). Apply glue liberally to straight edges of cork pieces and place cork against the back sticks, leaving the stick ends extended as shown.

Glue 14 sticks to the curved front edges of the cork.

Drill a small hole in one end of a stick and glue the stick to the back of the holder for hanging.

Holder can be made deeper by extending length of cork pieces and adding more sticks.

COUNTRY CHURCH

A child can easily and quickly assemble this little church if an adult will cut the cork pieces for him.

Paint the sticks in subdued shades to add a note of warmth, or spray the building with gold or silver to use with seasonal decorations.

Materials Needed:

38 sticks
Cork or plywood—8" x 5½"

Directions:

Cut cork or plywood using the patterns on the next page.

Place 10 sticks together, side by side, to form floor. Place cork or plywood in position about ¼" from ends of base sticks.

Apply glue to sides and tops and place side and roof sticks on. Overlap roof sticks where they join sides.

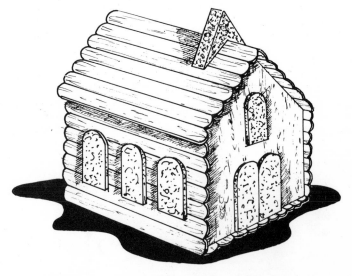

Cut doors and windows from cork or plywood using the patterns on the next page. Glue onto sides and front of church.

Cut a wedge for steeple. Make a "V" notch in long edge to fit the steeple over the roof point.

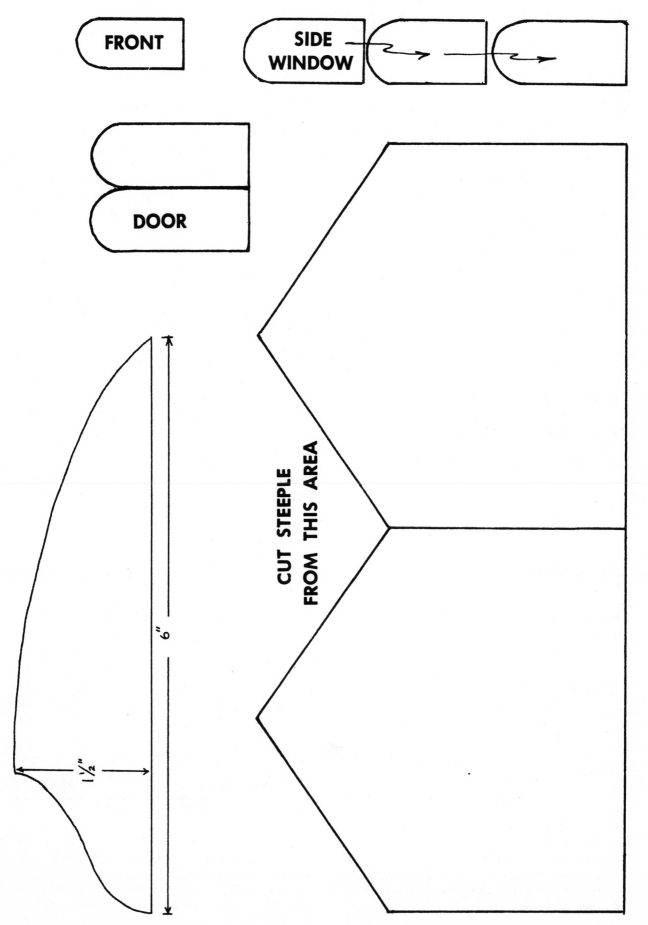

FRONT

SIDE WINDOW

DOOR

CUT STEEPLE FROM THIS AREA

6"

1½"

BIBLE BOX

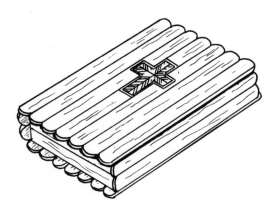

This easy-to-assemble Bible box can be used for Bible verses or Bible-school offerings.

Materials Needed:

22 craft sticks
Acrylic paint (black and red)
Two pieces of lightweight cardboard 2⅝″ x 4″
Two pieces of lightweight cardboard 4″ x ¾″
Two pieces of lightweight cardboard 2⅜″ x ¾″
Very lightweight interfacing 3½″ x 1″ (hinge)
Seal for front of Bible (cross, praying hands, head of Christ, etc., or see page 47)

Directions:

If you desire a product that does not have unfinished wood showing between the sticks, paint all craft sticks before you assemble them. For the Bible box, paint the inside "pages" red, and the outside black (or select your own colors).

Cut the rectangles 2⅜″ long from four craft sticks. Glue the craft sticks to the 2⅜″ x ¾″ pieces of lightweight cardboard. (You will find this is an easy way to glue craft sticks for a neater craft.)

The top and bottom of the Bible has seven craft sticks each. Glue them to the 2⅝″ x 4″ pieces of lightweight cardboard.

Glue two black craft sticks and two red craft sticks to the ¾″ x 4″ pieces of lightweight cardboard.

After the sticks are glued to the cardboards and are dry, glue the back (spine) of the Bible to the bottom. (see A).

Glue the top and bottom "pages" to the bottom (set in about ¼″ from the edges of the bottom of the Bible; see B).

Glue the "pages" edge (long side) to the bottom of the Bible (set in about ⅛″ from the edge; see C).

Set the top of the Bible in place, keeping all edges even. Glue the hinge to the top of the Bible and down over the back (see D).

When the hinge is dry, go over the glued area with black paint.

Inside the box, paint the top cardboard piece black and the sides and bottom pieces of cardboard red.

Glue the seal to the top of the Bible box.

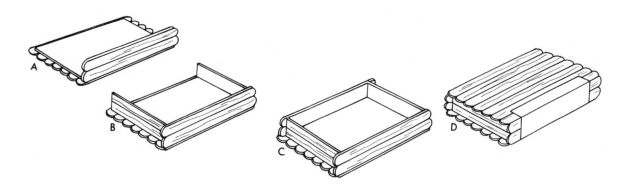

DECORATIVE CROSS

When sprayed with gold or silver, this cross becomes an especially usable decoration at Easter or Christmas time. Complement the cross with a touch of trailing ivy or an arrangement of greenery.

Materials Needed:

17 sticks

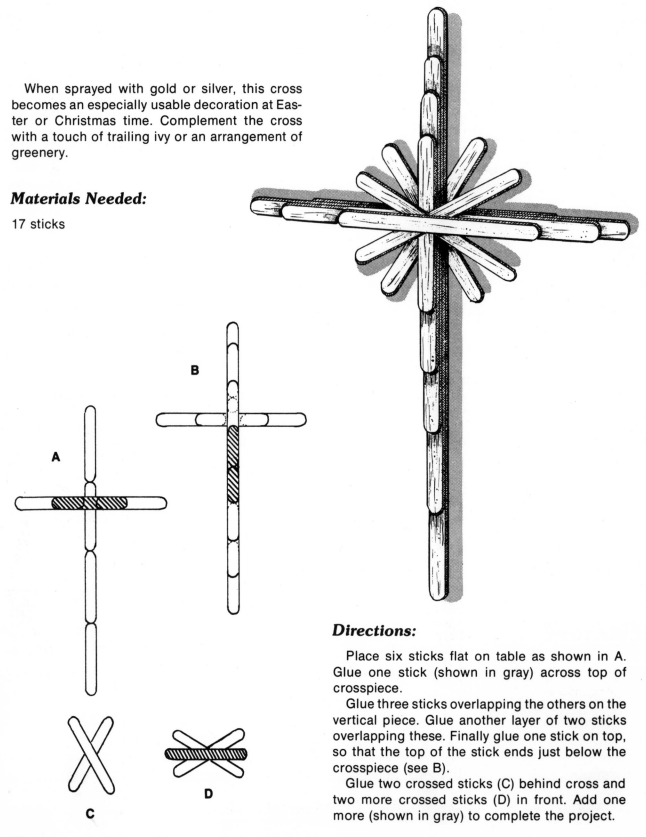

Directions:

Place six sticks flat on table as shown in A. Glue one stick (shown in gray) across top of crosspiece.

Glue three sticks overlapping the others on the vertical piece. Glue another layer of two sticks overlapping these. Finally glue one stick on top, so that the top of the stick ends just below the crosspiece (see B).

Glue two crossed sticks (C) behind cross and two more crossed sticks (D) in front. Add one more (shown in gray) to complete the project.

OLD TESTAMENT TEACHING AIDS

TABLETS WITH TEN COMMANDMENTS:

Secure parts of two sticks within base made of sticks or cork.

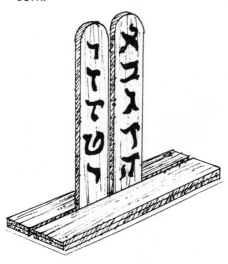

TORAH:

Glue ends of paper to sides of sticks. Roll toward center.

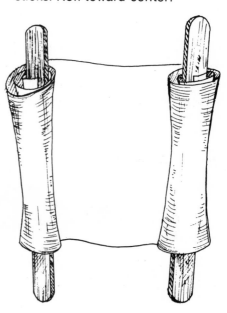

SCALES FOR JUSTICE:

Glue on half pieces

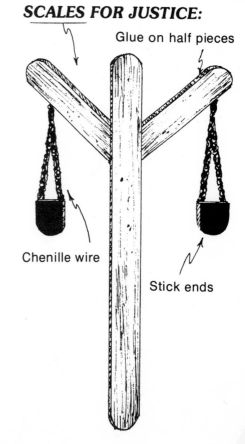

Chenille wire

Stick ends

MENORAH:

Push tiny beads (about ⅜″ diameter) onto pieces of chenille wire and glue to back of stick.

Place stick in stand of four sticks reinforced with two pieces of sticks.

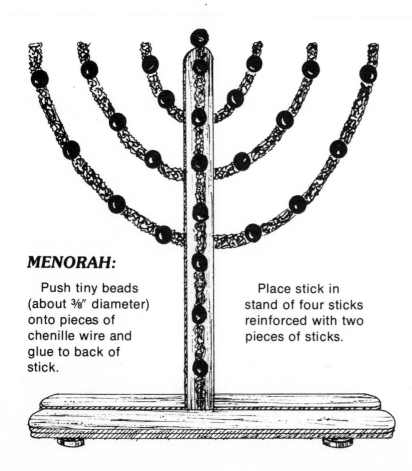

MESSAGE CENTER

This is a handy item to keep near the telephone or on the desk to jot down important messages and dates.

If the sticks are to be painted, this should be done before they are glued. After they are securely in place, and before the pen and note paper are added, the set can be varnished or shellacked.

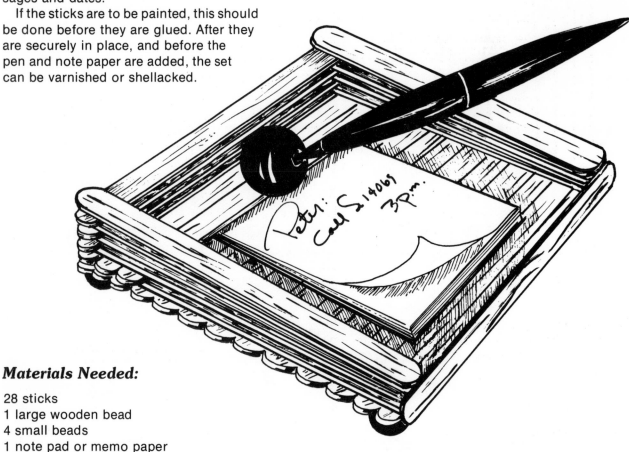

Materials Needed:

28 sticks
1 large wooden bead
4 small beads
1 note pad or memo paper
1 ball-point pen

Directions:

Place 11 sticks side by side. Glue on two cross sticks. See illustration (A).

Cement three sticks, parallel to first 11 sticks, across one end of cross sticks. Glue on two sticks as before (see side view). One end of the stick will be angled downward. Build three more layers adding one stick across the back and two side pieces angled down to the front, as shown in the side view.

Glue stick to front. (See illustration of finished project.)

Glue on large bead for pen holder and glue on four small beads for legs.

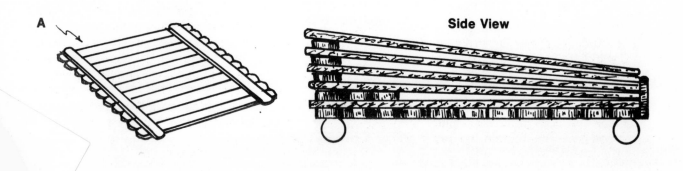

A

Side View

DESK SET

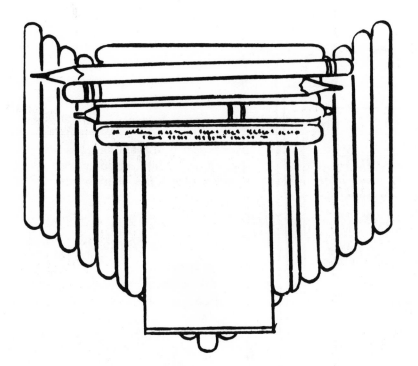

This easy-to-make desk set is great to keep for yourself, but handsomely designed to give away.

Materials Needed:

41 sticks
cardboard tube (4″ long)
varnish or paint
paint thinner
note pad

Directions:

Place 19 sticks together as shown (see A). Glue six sticks on top of the 19 sticks in the positions shown. This makes the base of the desk set.

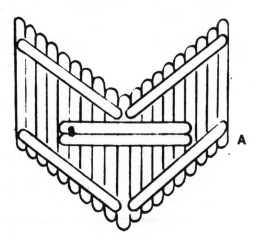

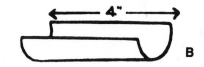

For the pencil holder, take the piece of cardboard tube (B) and glue five sticks on the top and six sticks on the bottom as in (C). Then glue a stick on each top edge as shown. (An additional stick may be needed on the back to help hold the top stick.)

Place the note pad into position and glue a stick on each side to hold the pad in place. (Op-

tional: Before gluing these sticks, 1¼″ can be cut from each stick using a razor saw so the pencil holder will rest more solidly on the base.)

Glue a stick on the center bottom of the pencil holder. Glue the holder to the base as shown.

Remove the note pad and varnish or paint.

Type or print Luke 11:9 (see page 47), or verse of your own choosing, on a thin strip of paper. When the set is dry, glue the verse on the front edge stick.

PENCIL HOLDER

This useful pencil holder is a constant reminder: Jesus is God's Son. Popular craft for children, welcome gift for any age.

Materials Needed:

39 sticks
1¼" x 1⅜" piece of cork.
Head of Christ seal (or illustration on page 47)
2¼" x 3½" piece of gold paper
1½" x 2½" piece of typing paper

Directions:

Place four sticks side by side. Glue three sticks on top of the four, as shown in (A). Make three more sets of these seven sticks.

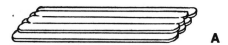

A

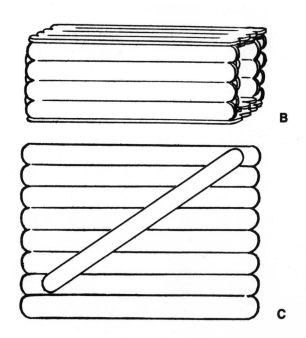

B

C

Glue the four sets of sticks together to form a box, as shown in (B). (You may need to give the child some extra help on this step.) Glue the small square of cork to bottom of box.

Place eight sticks side by side. Glue another stick diagonally across seven of the eight sticks (C). Glue the eighth stick side by side to the seventh stick. Glue two sticks directly on top of the eighth.

When the glue is dry, glue the panel of sticks to one side of the box of sticks.

Attach the head of Christ seal to the front of the box.

Type or print the verse, "Jesus is the Christ, the Son of God" (John 20:31), on the piece of typing paper, or use the verse printed on page 47. Glue the typing paper to the center of the gold paper, and then glue the gold paper to the panel.

TROUGH PLANTER

This rustic little planter can be lined with aluminum foil or thin tooling copper to hold live plants or flowers. It stands high enough to keep moisture from your table.

If you prefer a hanging planter, simply omit the legs and drill holes in each end for chain or rope hangers.

For a natural wood finish, apply a coat of varnish or shellac. For a bright color finish, apply a coat of lacquer or enamel.

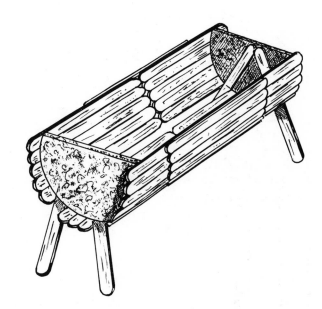

Materials Needed:

43 sticks
2 cork discs, 3″ diameter, ¼″ thick
(To make thinner cork discs into ¼″ thick ones, cement together.)

Directions:

Place two sticks end to end on your working table. Apply glue to one flat side of another stick and place stick over the other two.

Make 13 sets in the same way you made the first one (with three sticks). In all cases, the odd stick will be facing down when gluing to cork.

Apply glue to each set, ½″ from each end. Press cork onto stick set. Continue until all sets are glued to cork. Allow room for "leg" sticks as shown in illustration. Insert two sticks each end for legs, apply glue to hold them in position.

When you finish gluing the stick sets on, there will be five at each side and three at bottom.

When glue is thoroughly dry, trim cork at each side, as indicated by dotted lines.

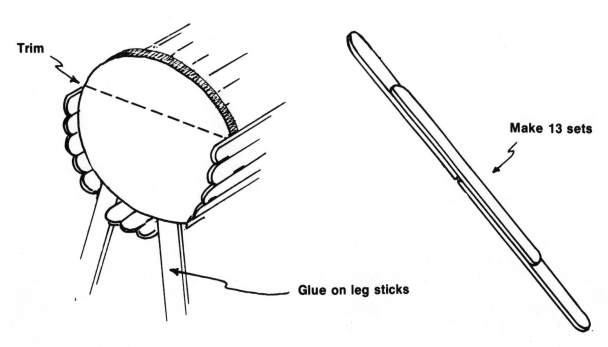

Trim

Glue on leg sticks

Make 13 sets

CHARIOT PLANTER

Here is a charming little planter that you will be proud to display. Add a touch of color to the wheels, line the planter with waterproof material and fill with soil.

Artificial leaves and flowers as well as small starts of live plants can be used.

Materials Needed:

62 sticks
3½" x 7" cork or thin plywood (¼" thick)

Directions:

Place 10 sticks together, side by side. Glue a stick over each end (A). Glue another stick over one end. Place two sticks over these (B).

Continue building in this way for at least six more layers, depending on the height desired. Cut and glue stick pieces to sides.

Turn the project over and glue on parts of sticks for handles. Cut one stick into three parts, and glue on as shown (C).

Cut two wheels of thin plywood or ¼" cork 3½" in diameter. Cut 1⅛" pieces from each end of eight sticks and glue eight onto each wheel.

Glue one wheel to each side of chariot.

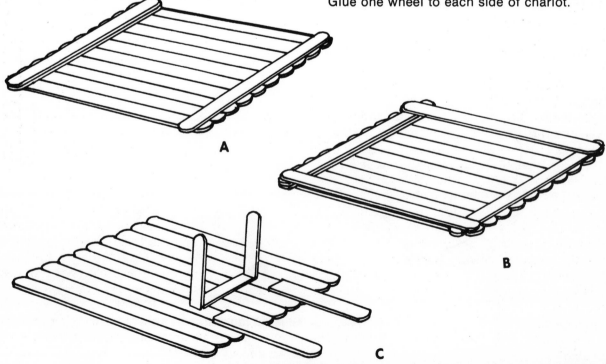

A

B

C

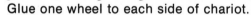

TEACHINGS OF JESUS PLAQUE

This plaque can be made as shown or changed to correlate with the lesson (Ten Commandments, etc.).

Materials Needed:

57 sticks
1 yard white or colored ½" ribbon
Macaroni letters
Chenille wire (same color as ribbon)
4 thumbtacks
Poster paint (if colored ribbon and chenille wire are used)
Varnish (optional)

Directions:

Lay two sticks flat and end to end. Spread glue on the flat side of another stick and lay this atop of the two sticks, parallel and in the middle (A). Make 13 of these double-length sticks.

Lay 11 of the double-length sticks side by side with the odd sticks up. Place one stick across each end of the 11 sticks, about ½" from each end (B). Figure B shows the back of the plaque. Turn the sticks over and place a stick across each end, about ¼" from ends.

Lay one of the remaining double sticks across the top and bottom of the front, odd sticks down, gluing them to the up and down sticks. Glue one stick on each end, even with the sticks below.

Glue two sticks together, in a "V" shape, with the sticks at the wide part approximately 2½" apart. Glue the sticks that will be used for a hanger to the back of the plaque.

On the remaining sticks put the following lines with macaroni letters, or use the lines printed on page 45: (1) Obey God's Laws; (2) Trust God; (3) Love God Best; (4) Trust Jesus; (5) Give to Jesus; (6) Be Honest; (7) Be Thankful; (8) Obey the Laws; (9) Seek the Lost; (10) Hear and Obey.

Cut the ribbon into four equal lengths (9" long). Cut one end of each piece diagonally. Glue the first stick approximately 5½" up from the diagonal edges of two pieces of ribbon. Glue the second through fifth sticks down the ribbon, approximately ½" apart. Repeat the process on the other two pieces of ribbon with sixth through tenth sticks.

Thumbtack the ribbon to the back of the plaque.

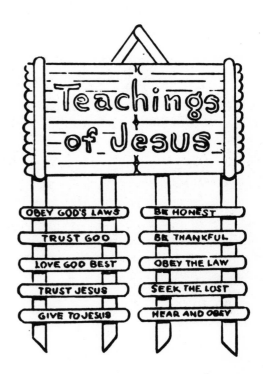

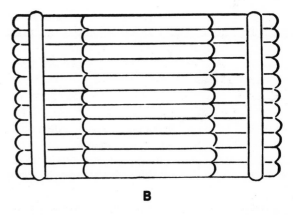

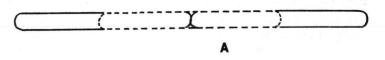

A

B

Bend pieces of chenille wire to form the words, "Teachings of Jesus," or use the lettering on page 45. Glue the letters on the plaque as shown.

If colored ribbon and chenille wire are used, paint the macaroni letters the same color.

If you wish to varnish the plaque, varnish the main part before the chenille wire is placed on it. Varnish the 10 single sticks before they are fastened to the ribbon.

UNIQUE PARTY FAVOR

This favor will perk up any party table, hospital tray, or banquet setting. Follow the colors suggested here, or choose your own.

Cover your working area with wax paper. You won't have to worry about the craft sticking to your working surface.

Materials Needed:

14 craft sticks
1 snap-apart skill stick
Acrylic paints (red, yellow, and green)
Black construction paper circle ½″ in diameter
Manila construction paper
Two ¼″ diameter beads
Toothpick
#484 Tacky cement
Paper mint cup or similar cup

Directions:

For base: Glue two pairs of craft sticks together (one on top of the other). Lay four craft sticks side by side. Glue together and let dry. Glue one set of two craft sticks to the four craft sticks (see A). Paint all craft sticks for base green.

For fence: Cut off the first joint of the snap-apart skill stick. Paint green. Paint three craft sticks yellow. Cut one craft stick in half.

Lay down snap-apart skill stick. Then lay down the two half raft sticks one inch out to either side. Keep the bottoms even (use flat ends for bottom). Put a dot of glue ⅝″ down from the top of the half sticks and one on the snap-apart stick at the same distance from the bottoms. Set a full length stick across and lightly press down, making sure you don't shift the sticks. Measure down about ½″ and put dots across all as before, setting the second full stick across the three posts. Allow fence to dry.

For birdhouse: Cut three craft sticks as shown (B) to form birdhouse. Cut small holding piece (1 3/16″) from craft stick. Paint these four pieces yellow (or color of your choice). Glue holding piece to back of birdhouse (see C).

Cut perch (D) and two pieces of roof (E). Paint green. Glue as shown to birdhouse.

Glue entrance hole above perch.

Glue the birdhouse to the top of the skill stick.

(End of skill stick should touch holding piece on back.)

For each bird (make two): Cut a piece of manila construction paper as shown (see F). Form the manila paper around a #3 double pointed knitting needle, starting at the large end. Tightly and evenly wind to the narrow end, sealing it with glue. This is the bird's body. Cut the body as diagramed (G) for the head and tail attachments.

Attach the bead onto the head end of the manila body with glue. Add a piece of toothpick to the bead to form the beak.

Cut the wings and tail from manila construction paper (see H and I). Attach with glue. Paint the birds red. Dot the eyes with yellow paint. Then add a black dot to center of yellow.

To put it all together: Set the double craft stick down and the rest of the base close to it. Glue the front and back tips of the fence posts and set them between the two. Let dry.

Glue the bottom of the paper mint cup to the top of the craft sticks, centered in front of the birdhouse, or if you wish, set the mint cup on it without being glued. (Small plastic cups can also be used. Sand lightly with fine sandpaper and paint, if desired. Sanding will help paint adhere.)

Glue the ⅝″ piece of craft stick (J) to the far left top of the fence (in front), to give the bird better gluing space. Attach the birds to the fence and perch with a generous drop of #484 Tacky cement.

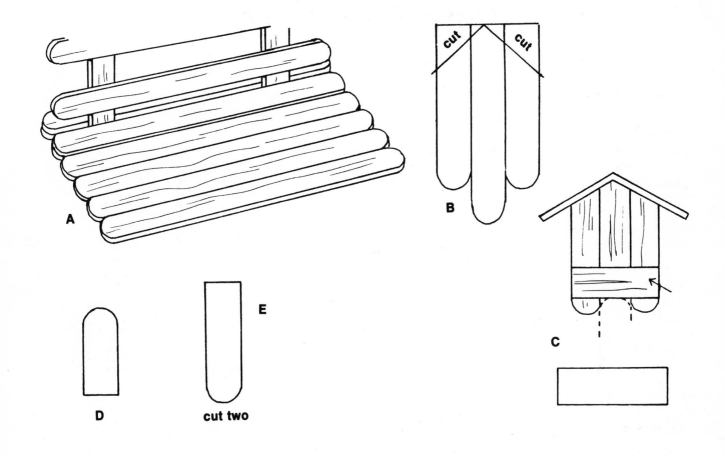

A

B

C

D

E

cut two

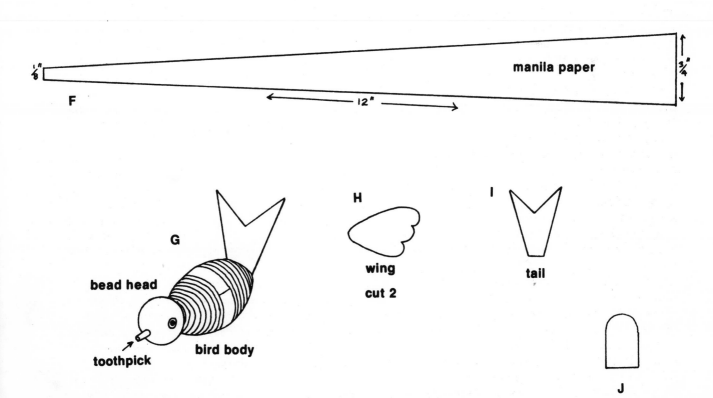

F

⅛" 12" ¾"

manila paper

G

bead head

toothpick

bird body

H

wing

cut 2

I

tail

J

STICK BASKETS

This basket is one of the craft stick favorites. It is not only easy to make, but the completed item has many uses around the home. A stick basket is an attractive server for fruits, potato chips, crackers, and rolls. It is also an ideal holder for bread slices.

The sticks are placed very close together, so any painting or staining should be done before they are glued. Apply shellac or varnish to the finished product with a spray can or gun.

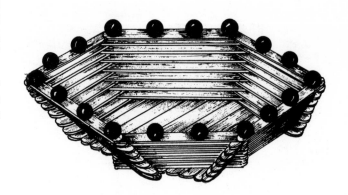

Materials Needed:

For 8″ basket—69 sticks, 18 ⅜″ beads
For 11″ basket—119 sticks, 24 ⅜″ beads

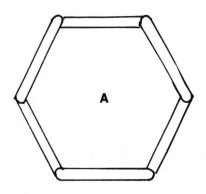

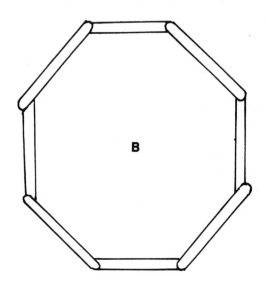

Directions (8″ basket):

Place six sticks down as shown (A). Apply glue where they overlap. Add another layer, overlapping sticks slightly. These sticks should be parallel to the first layer.

Continue adding layers, indenting sticks toward the center until basket is tall enough. (Remember, the shorter the sides, the shallower the basket.) At this point the space at the bottom should be narrow enough to fill in with a stick base. To make the base, glue sticks across the bottom of basket.

Directions (11″ basket):

Place eight sticks down as shown in (B). Follow procedure for the 8″ basket, building the sides and base in the same way.

Turn the basket right side up and decorate by gluing a bead to the end of every stick that shows on the rim, and adding more beads between them if desired.

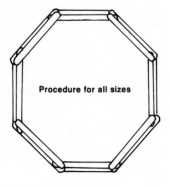

Procedure for all sizes

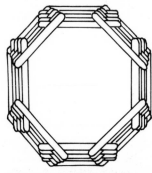

Will look like this after several layers

NOTE: In building stick baskets, it is advisable to build the structures without glue first to see how much you need to indent, particularly if this is your first attempt at basket-making.

SNACK BASKET

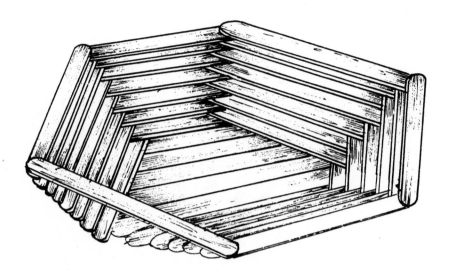

This graceful little server is useful as well as ornamental.

Materials Needed:

53 sticks

Directions:

Place six sticks down as shown (see A). Apply glue where sticks overlap.

Apply glue and place six more sticks onto the first layer (see B). Continue building, indenting sticks ½″ toward center, until there are eight sticks on each side.

When the sides are finished, there will be an open base to be filled by gluing five sticks across.

NOTE: Before you begin to glue, place all sticks in position to form the basket so you can be sure of correctly making it.

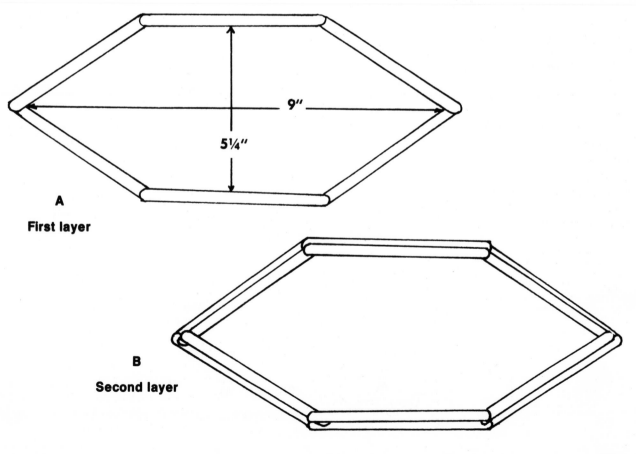

A

First layer

9″

5¼″

B

Second layer

HANGING PLANTER

This attractive container, filled with fresh flowers or a pretty plant, makes a lovely "special day" gift for a shut-in.

The sticks can be painted any color (preferably with enamel or lacquer) before being assembled. If you are using the planter for real leaves or flowers, line it with aluminum foil to make sure it is waterproof.

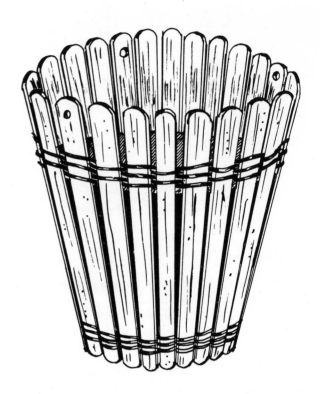

Materials Needed:

22 sticks
1 plastic bowl, waxed container or fiber planter bowl
Reed, plastic or cord

Directions:

Remove lid and rim of container so that sticks will lie flat against sides. Apply glue to one side of each stick, and arrange the sticks around the container so that they all touch. Sticks may overlap bottom of container ½", if desired. Spread the top ends of the sticks to allow a ¼" space between them. Be sure spaces between the top ends are even.

Drill holes in three sticks, placed at even distance apart, for attaching hanging cord.

Finally, weave cord in and out of the sticks.

If you have left the sticks in their natural state, give the finished project a coat of clear lacquer.

OWL FRIGIE

The owl frigie is a perfect note holder for your refrigerator.

Materials Needed:

11 craft sticks
Acrylic paint (brown and yellow)
2 black construction paper punched dots ¼" diameter
2 white construction paper circles ½" diameter
2 pieces magnetic tape 1" long
4" acrylic yarn (yellow, gray, or tan)
Rubber cement

Directions:

With wood-cutting shears, cut sticks as shown (see A-C).

A

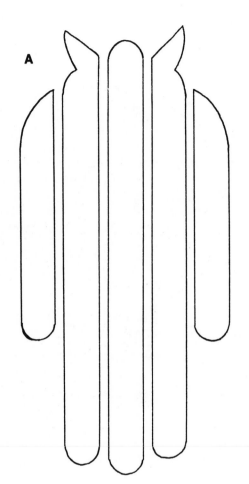

If you desire a finished product that doesn't have unfinished wood showing between the sticks, paint brown the sides and edges of all sticks before assembling. Allow to dry. With wood-cutting shears, cut sticks as shown.

Cut the beak as shown (see D) and paint yellow. (The beak can come from any leftover piece of craft stick.)

Cut the white circles and punch the black dots. Glue a black dot near the edge of each white circle.

Place the five cut body sticks side by side (see A). Glue the two straight pieces of stick to the back of the owl as shown (see E). These two cross sticks will hold the owl together.

When the owl is dry enough to pick up, turn it over. Glue the wings in place as shown. Glue the eyes in place just below the ears and keep them close to the outside edge of the head. Glue the beak just below the eyes.

Cut the yarn into ⅛" lengths. Place a liberal amount of glue just below the beak between the wings and down to the tip of the lower wing. Press the cut yarn into the glue.

When the owl is dry, turn it over and put rubber cement on the two cross sticks. Allow to dry. Remove the paper from the two pieces of magnetic tape and press them into the dried rubber cement.

B

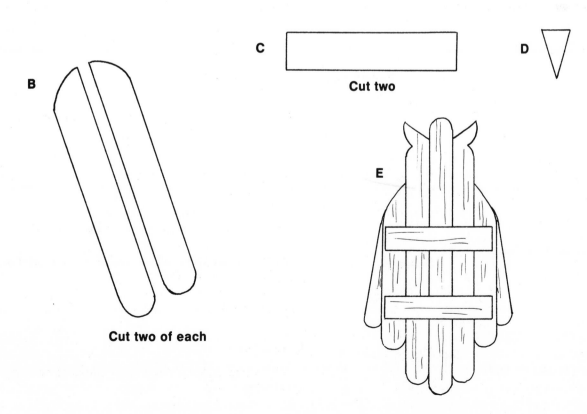

Cut two of each

C

Cut two

D

E

STAND-UP PICTURE

Select any Bible picture (2½″ x 3″) to complete this craft. If used as part of a Bible lesson, picture and lesson should correlate.

Materials Needed:

34 sticks
2½″ x 3″ Bible picture (If picture is not in color, provide crayons.)

Directions:

Place five sticks together side by side.

Glue four sticks on top of the five sticks, leaving space in center as shown in sketch.

Glue four more sticks on top of those, and then two more to the tops of the center two. This completes the base.

Lay 11 sticks side by side. Glue one stick across each end of the 11 sticks, about ½″ from the one end (bottom) and ¼″ from the other (top).

Turn the sticks over and glue the picture in the center. Glue two sticks over each side of the picture. Next, glue one stick across each end as on the back side.

Glue the framed picture in the slot in the base.

3-D MINI-SCENE

True worship comes from a heart full of praise and thanks. This easy-to-assemble craft will be a reminder to thank God for all of His many blessings.

Materials Needed:

15 sticks
Triangular background cut from greeting card or magazine
Mushroom, bird, and flower cut from greeting card or from page 47
"O Worship the Lord" printed on construction paper (or see page 47)
Wax shoe polish, soft cloth (optional)

Directions:

Glue three sticks in triangle shape. Glue on background art. Trim if necessary.

Continue building up remaining craft sticks into a frame. Glue at points where sticks overlap.

Glue flower between fourth and top craft stick on left. Glue bird on top left craft stick as if it is perched on the flower's stem. Glue mushroom between second and third craft sticks on bottom of the frame. Glue "O Worship the Lord" on bottom craft stick.

FLOWER VASE HOLDER

This easy-to-assemble vase will brighten any room when filled with a bouquet of fresh flowers. Consider making several to share with shut-ins.

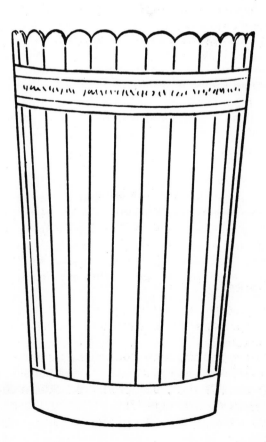

Materials Needed:

20-25 craft sticks
Tin jar lid
¼ cup Play-Doh
Glass to fit inside jar lid
30 inches of colored tape

Directions:

Knead Play-Doh and press into jar lid. Set glass in middle of Play-Doh.

Press craft sticks down into Play-Doh around glass. Keep as even as possible.

Place one row of colored tape around sticks about ½ inch from top. Place row of colored tape around inside of sticks. (Remove glass first.)

Spread glue around top of jar lid against sticks.

Circle edge of jar lid with colored tape.

3-D FISHING PICTURE

Four of Jesus' apostles were fishermen. Jesus invited them to "Follow me." This attractive 3-D picture reminds one and all to "follow Jesus daily."

Materials Needed:

18 craft sticks
1 wood stirring stick (mast)
6 snap-apart skill sticks
½ of a 1" Styrofoam ball
Corrugated cardboard 6½" x 8½" (background)
Corrugated cardboard 2" x 5" (boat bottom)
Acrylic paints (green, orange, brown, white, and two shades of blue)
Sobo glue
#484 Tacky cement (jar)
Yellow poster board 4" x 5" (sail)
Blue poster board 1¼" x ¾" (flag)
Lightweight cardboard 1" x 1⅝" (picture hanger)

Directions:

Cut all sticks to proper size with wood-cutting shears (see A-D). (Obtain a sharp pair of shears and reserve them for wood-cutting.) Paint boat sticks brown on all sides. Paint the stirring stick brown. (Do not paint back of stick.) If desired, paint frame sticks before assembly.

Cut Styrofoam ball as indicated in the pattern (see E). (Slice in half, then cut off the bottom of the half.) Paint it orange.

Cut boat bottom (see F) and background from corrugated cardboard using an X-Acto knife or an electric saber saw with a knife-edge blade. Paint boat bottom brown. Beginning at the bottom of the background, paint a green strip 1" high. Paint a dark blue strip 1⅛" high, leaving a middle section 3¼" for the boat to be painted brown. (This brown section on the dark blue strip starts 1¼" from the left side.) Paint the next 1⅛" strip light blue. The top section is painted white. With a near dry brush, make a light blue cloud in the upper right of the sky, using half circle strokes.

First layer of border: Place two craft sticks (uncut) along the left-hand side and two sticks along the right-hand side. Glue in place. At the top and bottom, center and glue an uncut craft stick. (There should be ⅝" gap on either side.)

Second layer: On left and right side, glue a craft stick on top of the two, centering it (gaps at both ends). Put two cut craft sticks, cut ends together, on top of the craft stick at the top and two others, cut and positioned, at the bottom.

Third layer: Glue two snap-apart skill sticks to the left-hand side and two skill sticks to the right-hand side. Center a skill stick to the top and one to the bottom. Glue in place (gaps at both sides).

Glue long boat sides and short ones along the corrugated boat bottom (see illustration). Glue two ⅞" stick pieces (see D) to inside of boat, across sticks at the back. Apply Tacky cement with a toothpick to inside front of boat to secure ends.

Glue sun in place, resting on the light blue water. With nearly dry brush, make sun reflection in sky and water with orange. (The sun should be about ½" from the side of the frame.)

Cut the flag from blue poster board and the sail from yellow poster board (see G and H).

Glue the blue flag to the top front of the mast. Glue the sail to the unpainted back of the mast. The bottom of the sail should be ¼" from the rounded tip of the mast. Glue the back of the mast and set it about ¾" down from the top frame and in from the left frame about 1⅝". The sail comes out to the right, toward the pointed end of the boat. The bottom of the mast is setting nearly ¼" onto the background boat back. Glue boat in place over the brown background. Bend sail forward and glue tab to the inside on the front, so it will appear curved.

Letter "Follow Jesus Daily" on three lines above the sun with a narrow black felt-tip pen, or use the words printed on page 39.

Make a hanger from lightweight cardboard (see I). Score as shown. Glue to the back of the picture.

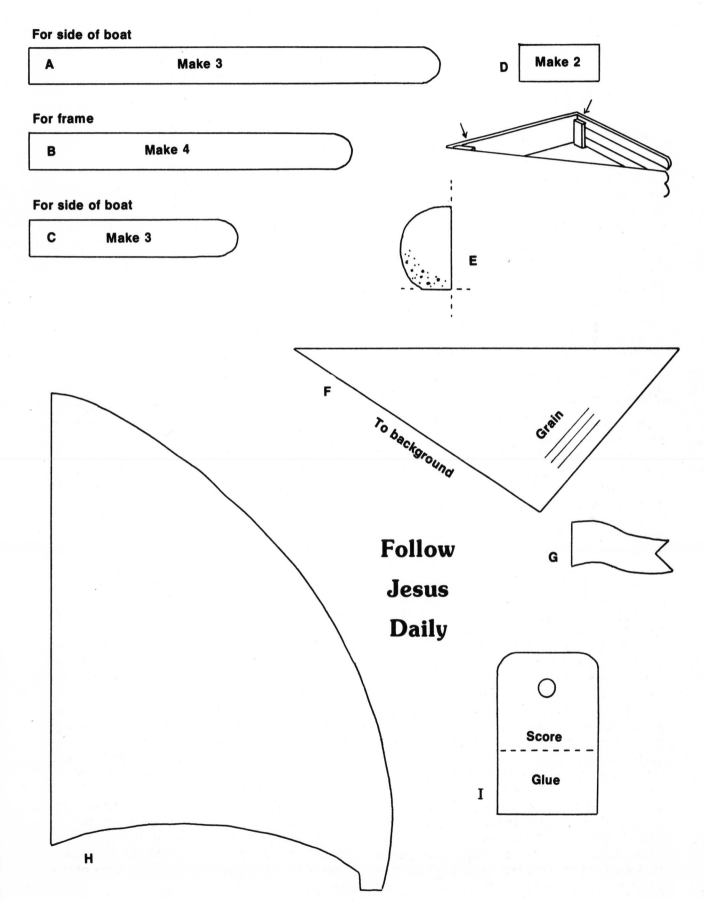

For side of boat

A   Make 3

For frame

B   Make 4

For side of boat

C   Make 3

D   Make 2

E

F

To background

Grain

Follow

Jesus

Daily

G

H

Score

Glue

I

TREASURE CHEST

Everyone needs a special place for treasures—whether the treasure is crayons or coins, stones or jewels. Finished in walnut stain with a coat of clear varnish, the chest becomes a shiny masterpiece for anyone in the family.

Materials Needed:

28 sticks
2 small wooden beads
1 yard gold plastic lacing
Cork pieces—5½" x 3⅝" x ¼" thick (or glue thinner cork pieces together)

Directions:

Place five sticks together, side by side.

Cut cork into side pieces, using the pattern on page 45. Make two pieces for each side (see illustration). Brush glue on the bottom (narrow) edges of lower pieces, and place onto sticks, 1/16" in from the ends.

Glue six sticks to each side of the cork ends. When glue is dry, cut small slits in each cork piece to attach handle of plastic lacing.

For lid, glue the other sticks around the cork half-circles.

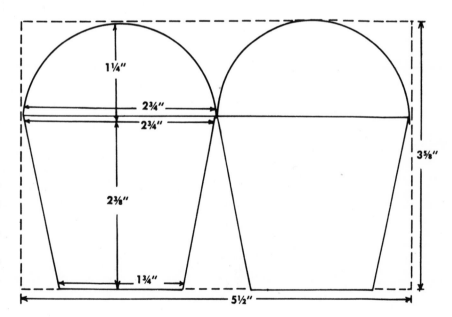

Place lid on box and glue on two rows of plastic lacing beginning at lower back and ending at front edge on lid. The lacing will act as hinges to enable you to open the box.

Glue two beads to the front of the box, one to the lid and one to the lower part. Attach a rubber band or piece of elastic to the bead on the lid to slip over the other bead for fastening.

FIRESIDE LAMP

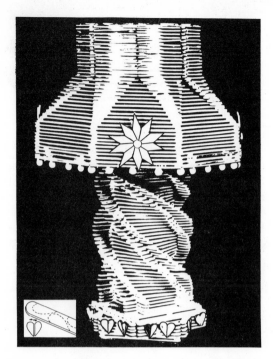

This beautiful, detailed lamp is worth the extra time and care needed for construction. Use the decoration suggestions shown or design your own.

Materials Needed:

Approximately 624 sticks
32 wooden beads
One 2¼″ wide x 7½″ long mailing tube or metal
    container

Directions for Base:

Fig. 1: Glue 11 sticks together, side by side (A). Glue three sticks across, one at each end, and one at center (B). Glue 11 more sticks across the three (C).

Fig. 2: Trim ends of four sticks (shown in gray on illustration), and glue them onto base, end to end.

Fig. 3: Glue four sticks around outside of trimmed sticks (D in Fig. 3).

Glue four sticks across base, as shown by black sticks. Build eight more layers (four sticks each) directly over layer D and layer shown in black.

Fig. 4: For top of base, build another base identical to Fig. 1. Top of this base is shown in gray on illustration. Glue top of base onto finished base.

Place two sticks onto base top, as shown by white sticks (Fig. 4). Place two more sticks onto base top as shown by black sticks in same illustration. Add six more layers until there are eight layers, as shown completed in Fig. 5.

Notch mailing tube to allow light cord to be pulled through. Glue mailing tube into the center of base. Push cord through base sticks as shown, and pull it through mailing tube.

Begin building spiral layers (two sticks in each layer). A spiral layer is built much the same as a square layer (shown in Fig. 5), but each stick is glued to the tip of the last stick with the other end allowed to indent ½″ (see black stick Fig. 5).

Build 73 spiral layers.

Fig. 6: Place two sticks on outside of each stick of last layer to support bulb fitting. Build three more layers in this way.

Drill corresponding holes through first two or three layers to secure lamp shade.

Directions for Shade:

Fig. 7: Whittle ends of four sticks (E), so that they can be placed into position with four more sticks as shown.

Build 21 4-stick layers directly on top of each other.

Glue on 28 layers, indenting half the width of a stick. Consult illustration (above) for result.

Build 28 more layers, directly on top of each other.

Fig. 8: Build four 6-stick supports as shown. These supports will be attached to shade, and screwed onto shade fitting.

Turn lamp shade upside down, so that bottom of shade is on top. Push the supports between layers on shade, as shown in Fig. 9. Apply a liberal coating of glue to ends and parts of supports (where they cross).

Drill corresponding holes in two supports, to attach shade fitting.

Fig. 10: Cut 10 wooden diamonds to pattern shown. Glue together to form flower. Make four flowers. Glue flowers to sides of shade.

Fig. 11: Cut 12 diamond-shaped pieces of wood. Glue three diamonds to each stick on top layer.

Glue beads around lower rim of shade.

Cut heart shapes from sticks and glue on (see photo above).

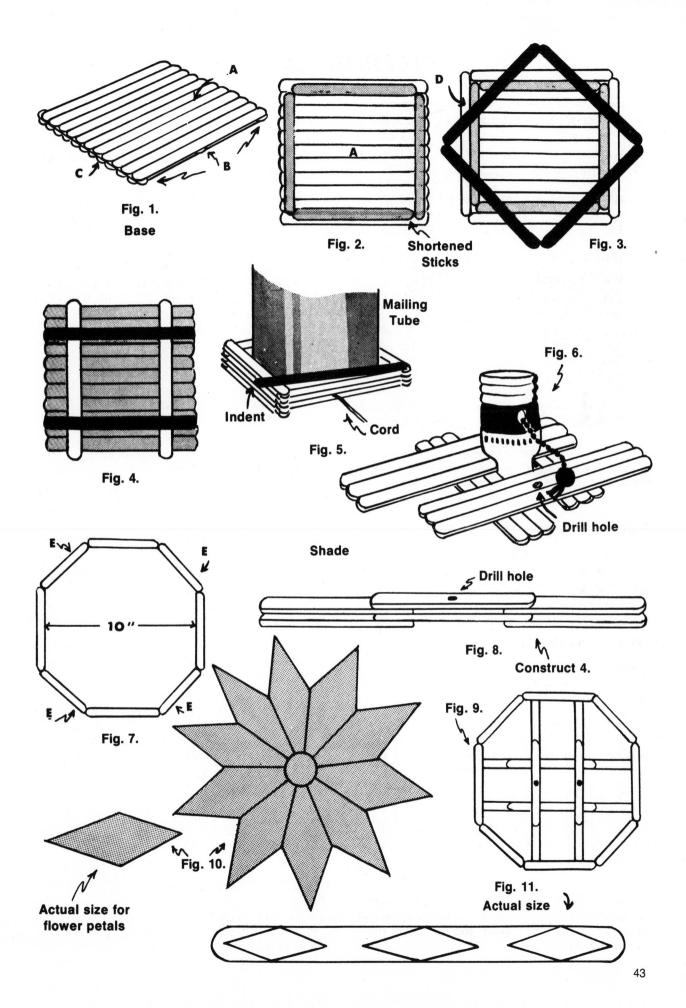

Fig. 1.
Base

A

C

B

Fig. 2.

A

Shortened Sticks

D

Fig. 3.

Fig. 4.

Mailing Tube

Indent

Cord

Fig. 5.

Fig. 6.

Drill hole

Shade

E

E

10"

E

E

Fig. 7.

Drill hole

Fig. 8.

Construct 4.

Fig. 9.

Fig. 10.

Actual size for flower petals

Fig. 11.
Actual size

43

BOWER

So simple to assemble that small children can build it, this charmingly old-fashioned type of wall decoration with its greeting card or magazine cutout will lend grace to any room in your home.

Apply a coat of clear varnish, decorate it with shells, tiny stones or artificial flowers, and this pretty bower will bring a touch of spring into your home.

Materials Needed:

22 sticks
Greeting card or magazine cutout (approximately 2½" x 4½")

Directions:

Back and Roof: Lay six sticks flat, side by side. Glue to front greeting card or magazine cutout. Place two sticks across ends (A) and (B). Place a third stick over stick ends at one end (C).

Glue on two sticks to form peaked roof. Glue sides of two sticks and place inside the first two. Add two more sticks outside the first two.

Stand: Glue two sticks together (braced by piece of stick) and glue over stick (B). Glue one more stick to this to form back.

Glue one stick over (C) and one to that to form stair. Glue on two more to make ledge for placing miniature flowers on.

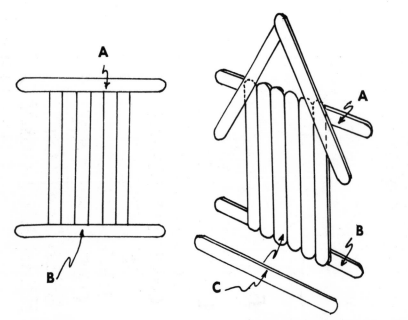

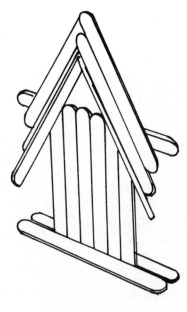

Teachings of Jesus

page 29

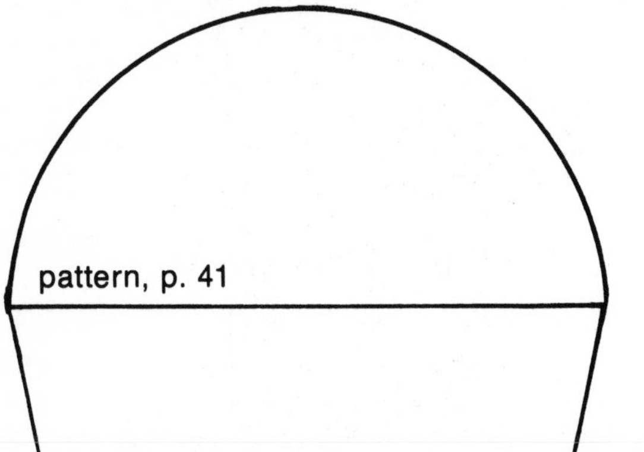

pattern, p. 41

pattern, p. 7

page 29

OBEY GOD'S LAWS
TRUST GOD
LOVE GOD BEST
TRUST JESUS
GIVE TO JESUS
BE HONEST
BE THANKFUL
OBEY THE LAW
SEEK THE LOST
HEAR AND OBEY

page 10

One-Dish
Meals
Cookbook